THIS BOOK BELONGS

Name: *Harry*

Favourite player: *Joe Lolly*

2020/2021

My Predictions...	Actual...

Forest's final position:

5	

Forest's top scorer:

Grabban	

Championship winners:

Wa?ord	

Championship top scorer:

Grabban	

FA Cup winners:

L.F.C	

EFL Cup winners:

No Sorist	

Contributors: Peter Rogers

A TWOCAN PUBLICATION

ISBN: 978-1-913362-33-1

£9

CONTENTS

TOBIAS 03
FIGUEIREDO

POSITION: Defender   **DOB:** 02/02/1994
COUNTRY: Portugal

Having initially joined Forest from Portuguese club Sporting in January 2018, central defender Tobias Figueiredo completed a permanent move to the City Ground in the summer of 2018 when he agreed a four-year contract with the Reds.

Figueiredo proved to be one of the mainstays of the Forest defence in 2019/20 when he made 34 appearances and scored three times for the side.

CYRUS 02
CHRISTIE

POSITION: Defender   **DOB:** 30/09/1992
COUNTRY: Republic of Ireland

Republic of Ireland international full-back Cyrus Christie joined Nottingham Forest on a season-long loan deal from Premier League new boys Fulham in September 2020.

A seasoned campaigner at Championship level, Christie has twice helped Fulham to win promotion to the Premier League. The 28-year-old defender began his career with Coventry City and also played for Derby County and Middlesbrough before moving to west London.

JOE 04
WORRALL

POSITION: Defender   **DOB:** 10/01/1997
COUNTRY: England

Another product of the Forest Academy, central defender Joe Worrall has benefitted from loan spells with Dagenham and Redbridge plus a stint with Scottish giants Glasgow Rangers earlier in his career.

Now back at the City Ground, Worrall enjoyed an ever-present 2019/20 campaign and has gained a reputation as one of the very best defenders outside of the Premier League.

LUKE
FREEMAN

SOCCER SKILLS

Great goalkeepers are an essential ingredient for successful teams in today's game. They have to excel in all areas of the art of 'keeping and Brice Samba is a great 'keeper that lives up to these expectations.

DISTRIBUTION
THE BASICS OF GOOD THROWING TECHNIQUE

OVERARM THROW

This is best for covering long distances. The body should be in line with the direction of the throw with the weight on the back foot. The ball should be brought forward in a bowling action with the arm straight.

JAVELIN THROW

This throw is made quickly with a low trajectory. The arm is bent for this throw, the ball is held beside the head and the body is in line with the direction of the throw. The arm is brought forward in a pushing movement with the ball being released at the top.

UNDERARM THROW

The ball is released from a crouching position, with a smooth underarm swing.

Throws do not usually travel as far as kicks but the greater speed and accuracy of throwing can make up for the lack of distance and will help the team retain possession. A player receiving a throw must be able to control it early.

Work hard at distribution and the benefits of this will be seen whenever you are in possession during a match.

EXERCISE ONE

Grab a friend and throw the ball to each other using the various throwing techniques at various distances apart.

EXERCISE TWO

The goalkeeper with the ball uses the various throws to knock another ball off a marker.

EXERCISE THREE

The goalkeepers try to throw the ball through the markers using various throwing techniques.

BOYS OF 1979

Nottingham Forest began the 1978/79 season as reigning First Division champions and ended a historic campaign with three trophies in the City Ground trophy cabinet.

The campaign began with Forest thumping FA Cup winners Ipswich Town 5-0 in the Charity Shield at Wembley. After securing the first piece of silverware in the season's curtain raiser, Forest went on to win the League Cup at Wembley before recording a fabulous European Cup triumph.

Not only did Brian Clough's men secure the Charity Shield and cup double but they also pushed Liverpool all the way in the First Division title race before finishing the campaign as runners-up.

Victories over Oldham Athletic, Oxford United, Everton, Brighton and Watford landed Forest a Wembley date with Southampton in the League Cup final. Goals from Gary Birtles (2) and Tony Woodcock saw Forest defeat the Saints and secure their second piece of silverware of the season.

JOHN ROBERTSON

Widely regarded as the finest Nottingham Forest player of all time, Scottish international midfielder John Robertson was once again a star performer in Brian Clough's formidable 1978/79 team.

The skilful left-winger was blessed with great close control and outstanding ability to cross a ball with pin-point accuracy. He was one of the first names on Clough's teamsheet throughout his career at the City Ground and was ever-present in the 1979/80 season.

Famed for crossing the ball for Trevor Francis' winning goal in the 1979 European Cup final triumph, Robertson was on target himself in the semi-final first leg victory over FC Koln and also netted four goals in the successful League Cup campaign.

It was the team's European Cup success that really caught the fans' imagination as Forest defeated Liverpool in the first round in a match dubbed the 'Battle of Britain'. Next up were memorable victories over AEK Athens, Grasshopper and FC Koln before Clough's men faced Swedish side Malmo in a Munich final.

Malmo were a well organised and defensively minded outfit that Clough's men found hard to break down. However, as the first half drew to a close, John Robertson picked the perfect moment to beat two defenders down the left before whipping in an inviting cross to the far post where Trevor Francis was perfectly placed to head home the only goal of the game. Nottingham Forest were champions of Europe!

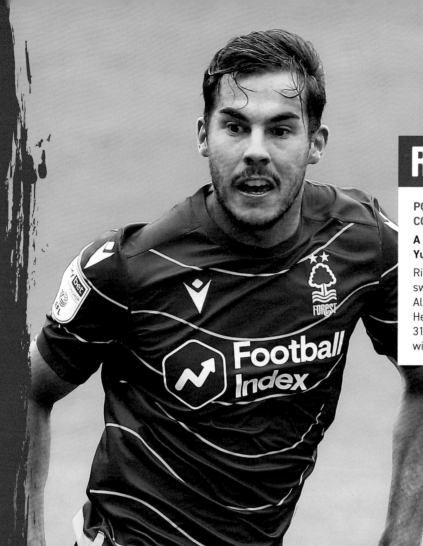

05 YURI RIBEIRO

POSITION: Defender **DOB:** 24/01/1997
COUNTRY: Portugal

A former Portugal under-21 international, left-back Yuri Ribeiro joined the Reds in July 2019 from Benfica.

Ribeiro arrived in Nottingham, having agreed a permanent switch to the City Ground, along with Benfica teammate Alfa Semedo who joined on a season-long loan deal. He produced a number of polished performances during 31 first team appearances in his debut season with the club.

06 LOIC MBE SOH

POSITION: Defender **DOB:** 13/06/2001
COUNTRY: France

Nottingham Forest completed the signing of 19-year-old French youth international Loic Mbe Soh on the eve of the new 2020/21 Sky Bet Championship campaign.

A highly-promising central defender, Mbe Soh was signed from Paris Saint-Germain and also provides the flexibility of being able to operate at right-back. Mbe Soh has represented his country at various youth levels and has previously captained the French national under-18 team.

TEAM 2020/21

LEWIS 07 GRABBAN

POSITION: Striker **DOB:** 12/01/1988
COUNTRY: England

Lewis Grabban enhanced his reputation as one of the Championship's most feared strikers by hitting the 20-goal mark for Forest in 2019/20.

The much-travelled frontman netted a brace against one of his former clubs as Forest drew 2-2 away to Millwall in December 2019. His goal tally saw him land the runners-up spot in the club's Player of the Season voting at the end of the season.

08 JACK COLBACK

POSITION: Midfielder **DOB:** 24/10/1989
COUNTRY: England

After making 55 appearances in a Forest shirt during his loan deals at the City Ground over the last two seasons, midfielder Jack Colback joined the club on a permanent basis in the summer of 2020 following his release from Newcastle United.

Blessed with great experience following his time at St James' Park plus spells with Sunderland and Ipswich Town (on loan), Colback's committed performances have made him a popular figure with Forest fans.

PREPARING
FOR ACTION

Football matches may well be scheduled for 90 minutes but there are many days of preparation that go into making sure that Chris Hughton's men are at their physical and mental peak when they cross the white line to represent Nottingham Forest Football Club.

Like all Championship clubs, Forest's pre-match planning is meticulous. The manager of course has final say as to who makes his starting line-up but the boss is ably assisted by a backroom staff of coaches, sports scientists, strength and conditioning experts, physiotherapists and nutritionists who all play their part in helping fine tune the players ahead of the manager's team selection.

The majority of the squads' preparations take place at the club's training ground and that all begins when the players report back for pre-season training.

Although the modern-day player has little down-time in terms of maintaining his overall fitness, pre-season really is a vital time for footballers to build themselves up to remain as fit, strong and healthy as possible for the challenging season that awaits.

The pre-season schedule often begins with a series of fitness tests. The results of those tests enables the club's coaching and fitness staff to assess each player's condition and level of fitness to ensure they are given the right work load during the pre-season programme.

When it comes to winning football matches, it is well known that both hard work and practice are two essential ingredients to success. However, in terms of strength and fitness, then rest, recovery and diet also have crucial parts to play in a footballer's wellbeing.

The modern game now sees technology playing its part in training too - prior to beginning their training sessions, the players are provided with a GPS tracking system and heart rate analysis monitors ensuring that all that they do in a training session can be measured, monitored and reviewed.

On-pitch training drills and gym work is now enhanced further with players often taking part in yoga and pilates classes while always receiving expert advice in terms of their diet, rest and mental welfare.

Challenge your favourite grown-up and find out which of you is the biggest Championship brain!

ADULTS

Who is the only Championship club to have won the Premier League?

1 Hull City

How many teams in the 2020/21 Championship have never competed in the Premier League?

2 Luton Fulham

Which former Leeds United and Norwich City midfielder currently plays for Middlesbrough?

3 ANSWER

At which Scottish club was QPR manager Mark Warburton once in charge?

4

Blackburn Rovers' manager Tony Mowbray previous played for and managed which Championship rival?

5 ANSWER

At which club did Sheffield Wednesday manager Garry Monk begin his managerial career?

6 ANSWER

From which club did Boro sign striker Britt Assombalonga?

7 ANSWER

Millwall manager Gary Rowett previously played for the Lions - true or false?

8 ANSWER

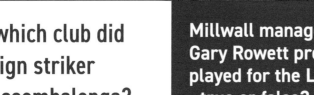

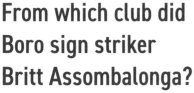

At which Championship ground will you find the Invincibles Stand?

9 ANSWER

In which year did Steve Cooper become Swansea City manager?

10 ANSWER

V KIDS

The adults' questions are on the left page and the kids' questions are on the right page.

Which Championship club play their home games at Carrow Road?

1

What is Sheffield Wednesday's nickname?

2

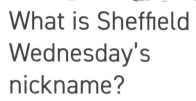

Which two clubs won automatic promotion to the Championship in 2019/20?

3

Ashton Gate is home to which Championship club?

4

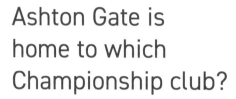

Who is the manager of Cardiff City?

5

How many Welsh clubs are competing in the 2020/21 Championship?

6

Mark Warburton is the manager of which Championship team?

7

Which Championship stadium has the largest capacity?

8

How many Championship clubs have the word 'City' in their name?

9

What nationality is Preston manager Alex Neil?

10

17

ANSWERS ON PAGE 62

Fill the page with your footy goals and dreams, no matter how big or small, and then start working on how to accomplish them!

We've started you off...

1. Visit the City Ground

2. Complete 50 keepy-uppies

FOOTY BUCKET LIST

SAMBA
SOW

ANSWERS ON PAGE 62

WHO ARE YER?

Can you figure out the identity of all these Forest stars?

FOREST

11 SAMMY AMEOBI

POSITION: Midfielder **DOB:** 01/05/1992
COUNTRY: England

An experienced and attack minded midfielder, Sammy Ameobi joined Forest in the summer of 2019 following a three-year spell with Bolton Wanderers.

Ameobi went on to feature in 48 first team fixtures during his first season at the City Ground and netted five Championship goals. Among his 2019/20 strikes was the opening goal in the 2-0 victory over champions-elect Leeds United in February 2020 plus a brace the 2-2 draw at home to Swansea City in July.

JORDAN 12 SMITH

POSITION: Goalkeeper **DOB:** 08/12/1994
COUNTRY: England

Goalkeeper Jordan Smith has now made over half a century of appearances for the Reds since making his first team debut away to Norwich City back in February 2017.

A product of the club's Academy, Smith proved to be a reliable understudy to Brice Samba throughout the 2019/20 campaign. He played in the FA Cup third round tie at Chelsea and also featured in two league fixtures at the end of the campaign.

14 FOUAD BACHIROU

POSITION: Midfielder **DOB:** 15/04/1990
COUNTRY: Comoros

Forest completed the signing of Malmo midfielder Fouad Bachirou just a couple of weeks ahead of the new 2020/21 Sky Bet Championship campaign.

The much-travelled 30-year-old, who has experience of both Champions League and Europa League football, arrived at the City Ground having previously plied his trade in France with Paris Saint-Germain, in Scotland with Greenock Morton and also in Sweden with successful spells at Ostersunds and Malmo.

LUKE 15 FREEMAN

POSITION: Midfielder **DOB:** 22/03/1992
COUNTRY: England

Attacking midfielder Luke Freeman joined Nottingham Forest on a one-year loan deal from Premier League Sheffield United in August 2020.

An instrumental player at Championship level with both Bristol City and Queens Park Rangers, his arrival at the City Ground gives the team further attacking options for the 2020/21 campaign. His loan move to Forest also has an option to become a permanent deal.

BOYS OF 1959

Under the guidance of long serving manager Billy Walker, Nottingham Forest completed their 1958/59 campaign with an FA Cup final victory over First Division rivals Luton Town.

After winning promotion from the Second Division in 1956/57, Forest once again secured a mid-table top-flight finish by ending the season in 13th place with 40 points. They may have dropped two places and two points from their 1957/58 achievement of eleventh place and 42 points but the Reds really made their mark in the FA Cup.

Their bid to land the FA Cup for a second time, having first won the famous old trophy back in 1898, began with a third-round victory over non-league Tooting & Mitcham. The initial meeting with the Minnows ended 2-2 but Forest ran out comfortable 3-0 winners in the City Ground replay.

A 4-1 fourth-round victory at home to Grimsby Town was followed by another home tie in round five. After being held to a 1-1 draw by Birmingham City, Forest turned on the style

THOMAS WILSON

A prolific marksman for the Reds throughout the 1950s, Thomas Wilson scored six goals in the club's successful 1958/59 FA Cup campaign.

Having joined Forest from his local side Cinderhill Colliery in 1951, Wilson was converted from a winger to a centre-forward and went on to score 14 goals in 1956/57 as the Reds won promotion from the Second Division to the top flight.

The 1958/59 season was Wilson's most prolific campaign at the City Ground and saw him net 21 First Division goals plus a further six in the FA Cup including the second in the Wembley final.

His goal at Wembley proved to be the winner and has subsequently etched his name into Nottingham Forest folklore.

in the replay at St Andrew's to register a 5-0 win and book a quarter-final tie at home to Bolton Wanderers.

Forest edged past Wanderers 2-1 in the quarter-final and then defeated Aston Villa 1-0 in the semi-final at Hillsborough to secure the club's first ever trip to Wembley.

In front of 100,000 at Wembley, Walker's men made a flying start to the showpiece final against Luton Town as goals from Roy Dwight and Tommy Wilson gave them a 2-0 lead inside the opening 14 minutes.

Dwight's afternoon sadly went from ecstasy to agony as he was stretchered off with a broken leg after 33 minutes. With no substitutes in those days, Forest battled on with ten men. Despite the Hatters pulling a goal back in the second half, the ten men stood strong and ensured the Cup headed to the City Ground following a 2-1 Wembley triumph.

FOREST

LYLE

TAYLOR

SOCCER SKILLS

DEFENDING

Defending is an art - not as spectacular as swerving a free kick around the wall into the net or floating a crossfield pass into the path of an oncoming wingback - but nevertheless, just as important. Every successful team has a solid defence and can defend as a team.

Defenders must also master the art of defending one on one...

EXERCISE ONE

Two adjacent 10m x 10m grids have two players, X and Y at the opposite ends of the grids. X plays the ball to Y, who is then allowed to attack defender X with the ball. Y's target is to be able to stop the ball, under control, on the opposite end line. Defender X has to try to stop this happening. Y is encouraged to be direct and run at X with the ball.

KEY FACTORS

1. Do not approach the attacker square on. Adopt a sideways stance which enables rapid forward and backwards movement.

2. Do not dive in. Be patient and wait for your opponent to make a mistake. Always be on your toes.

3. Threaten the ball without actually committing to a tackle. Pretending to tackle can often panic the opponent!

4. Tackle when you are sure you will win it!

EXERCISE TWO

Here the game is progressed to a two v two situation when X1 and X2 play as a team against Y1 and Y2.

The same target is used for this game - the players have to stand on the opposite line with the ball, either by dribbling past their opponents or by passing the ball through them.

The same key factors are relevant here with the addition of two more:

5. Covering your defending partner when he is being attacked.

6. Communication between the two defenders is vital.

If a team can get these points of defending right, throughout the side, they will become very difficult to beat.

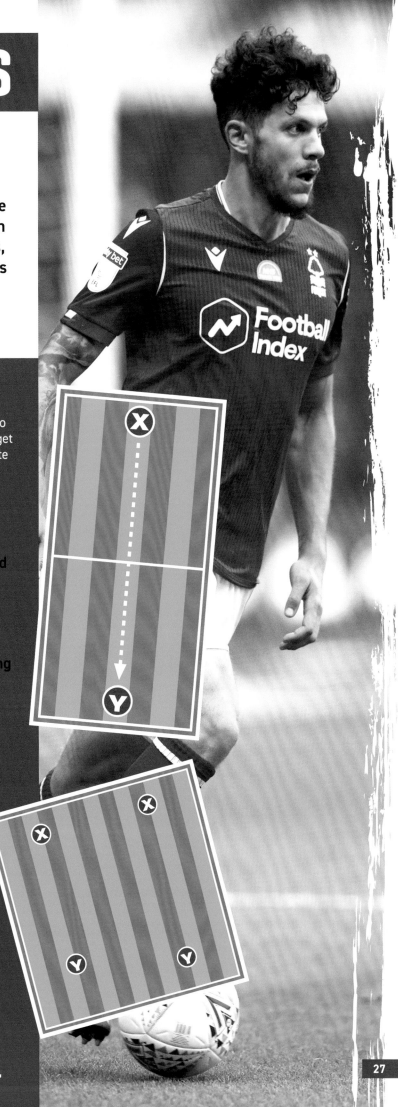

Take our quick-fire personality test to see where Chris Hughton would utilise your skills in the Forest line-up...

WHICH FOOTBALLER ARE YOU?

1. What is your favourite activity at the park?

a. Leaping around
b. Practicing my heading
c. Lots of non-stop running
d. Scoring goals

2. What is your biggest strength?

a. My height
b. My strength
c. My stamina
d. My speed

3. Which would you rather win?

a. A game of catch
b. A weight lifting contest
c. A long distance run
d. A sprint race

4. You score a goal! How do you celebrate?

a. I turn and punch the air
b. I clench my fist in delight
c. I high-five a teammate
d. I slide on my knees

5. How would the opposition describe you?

a. Hard to beat
b. Determined to succeed
c. All-action
d. Lethal in front of goal

6. What's your favourite move?

a. Springing high to catch under pressure
b. A sliding tackle
c. Playing the perfect through ball
d. Spinning away from my marker

7. What is the key to winning a game?

a. Keeping a clean sheet

b. Winning your individual battles

c. Maintaining possession

d. Taking chances that come your way

MOSTLY As

You would clearly be a safe pair of hands in goal. Watch out Brice Samba, there's competition here!

8. What is your favourite number?

a. One

b. Five

c. Seven

d. Nine

MOSTLY Bs

Sounds like you are a young Yuri Ribeiro in the making - there could well be a role for you in the Forest back four...

MOSTLY Cs

You could comfortably take your place in the heart of midfield and help make things tick. Move over Sammy Ameobi!

9. How would you describe your style of play?

a. Disciplined

b. Fully committed

c. Relentless

d. Technically gifted

10. What do your teammates call you?

a. Secure

b. Reliable

c. Energetic

d. Mr/Miss goals

MOSTLY Ds

Looks like we have a budding Lewis Grabban on our hands! Who do you fancy partnering in attack?

FOREST

CARL 16 JENKINSON

POSITION: Defender **DOB:** 08/02/1992
COUNTRY: England

Former England under-21 international right-back Carl Jenkinson joined Nottingham Forest in August 2019 from Arsenal.

After making his league debut for the Reds away to one of his former clubs, Charlton Athletic, a combination of injuries and the performances of Matty Cash in the right-back berth limited Jenkinson to ten first team appearances in all competitions last season. A quality defender, Jenkinson will be hopeful of more first team action in 2020/21.

17 ALEX MIGHTEN

POSITION: Striker **DOB:** 11/04/2002
COUNTRY: England

Exciting young winger Alex Mighten gave Forest fans a big boost ahead of the 2020/21 season when he agreed a new long-term deal keeping him at the City Ground until the summer of 2025.

After tasting cup action against London giants Arsenal and Chelsea last season, the England youth international also featured in eight Championship fixtures in a breakthrough season for the Nottingham-born Academy starlet.

MIGUEL 19 ANGEL GUERRERO

POSITION: Striker **DOB:** 12/07/1990
COUNTRY: Spain

Spanish striker Miguel Angel Guerrero became the sixth new face at the City Ground ahead of the new 2020/21 Sky Bet Championship campaign.

The 30-year-old front man arrived Trentside from Greek club Olympiacos and boasts both Champions League and Europa League experience. A much-travelled goal getter, he will add to the competition for a place in the Reds' frontline.

20 MICHAEL DAWSON

POSITION: Defender **DOB:** 18/11/1993
COUNTRY: England

Central defender Michael Dawson now has over a century of league appearances for Forest under his belt across two separate spells at the City Ground.

His vast experience has become a vital ingredient in the Forest squad and in June 2020 he agreed to remain at the club for a further year. Dawson began his career with Forest before enjoying lengthy spells with Tottenham Hotspur and Hull City. The England international returned to the club in the summer of 2018.

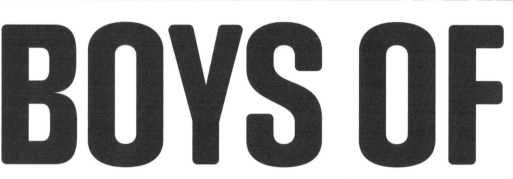

BOYS OF 1989

Forest went in search of silverware on four fronts in 1988/89 and enjoyed two triumphant trips to Wembley.

Brian Clough's highly entertaining side had a marvellous season on the cup front, winning the both the League Cup and the Full Members Cup before bowing out of the FA Cup against Liverpool at the semi-final stage. In total Forest played in a mammoth 20 cup ties in 1988/89 and still managed to find the stamina to secure a third-place finish in the First Division.

Forest's quest for a third League Cup triumph began with a comprehensive 10-0 aggregate victory over Chester City before seeing off Coventry City, Leicester City and Queens Park Rangers to tee-up a semi-final date with Bristol City.

STAR PERFORMER
STUART PEARCE

All-action left-back Stuart Pearce had an outstanding season in 1988/89 for both club and country.

At the City Ground he became recognised as one of football's most inspirational and inspired skippers. In a season that saw him lift two trophies at Wembley, Pearce also reached double figures in the goal charts with his explosive free-kicks becoming something of a trademark for him and a dread for opposition goalkeepers.

On the international scene, Pearce featured in all of England's games during the season to firmly establish himself as the country's first choice left-back.

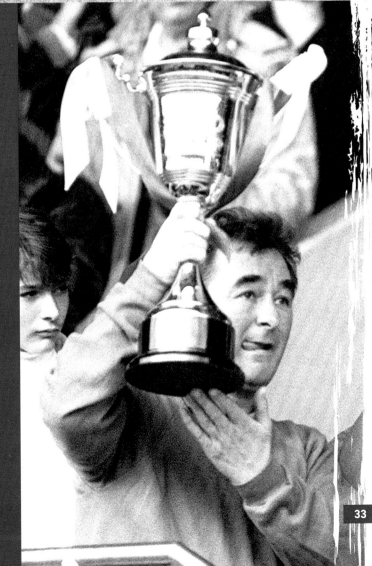

After overcoming the Robins, they faced League Cup holders Luton Town in the Wembley final. Trailing 1-0 at the break, Forest produced a sensational second-half showing with goals from Neil Webb and a Nigel Clough brace sealing a 3-1 victory.

Having won the League Cup at Wembley on 9 April, Clough's men returned to the Twin Towers again before the month was out to face Everton in the Full Members Cup final on 30 April. Lee Chapman and Garry Parker both scored twice as Forest ran out 4-3 winners after extra-time.

The level of quality in Forest's 1988/89 squad was demonstrated by five players being called up to play for England; captain Stuart Pearce, Des Walker, Steve Hodge, Neil Webb and Nigel Clough.

FOREST

Football Index

COLOUR

TYLER

BLACKETT

LEWIS
GRABBAN

PLAYER OF
THE SEASON

MATTY CASH

Matty Cash capped off five great years at the City Ground as he was crowned Nottingham Forest's Player of the Season once the Reds' eleven-month 2019/20 Sky Bet Championship campaign was finally concluded.

Chosen by the supporters, following an end-of-season vote, Cash's performances certainly made an impression on the City Ground faithful after he secured the prestigious award with 60 per cent of the vote. Striker Lewis Grabban was runner-up having topped the Forest scoring charts with 20 league goals in 2019/20, while goalkeeper Brice Samba was third following a highly impressive debut season at the City Ground.

Almost ever-present throughout last season, Cash featured in 42 of Forest's 46 Championship fixtures and enjoyed a highly consistent season for the Reds. With the ability to operate in midfield or at right-back, Cash's versatility was certainly of great benefit to the side.

The 23-year-old certainly wasted little time in making his mark on the 2019/20 campaign - Forest's season was just eight minutes old when he netted the club's first goal of the campaign on opening day against West Bromwich Albion. Cash was also on target in the return fixture in February 2020 when his last-minute equaliser secured a point following a 2-2 draw at the Hawthorns.

The Forest Academy graduate follows in the footsteps of club legends such as Garry Birtles, Nigel Clough, Des Walker and Stuart Pearce in winning the award, while taking the title from teammate Joe Lolley who landed the honour in 2018/19.

With 42 league appearances, three goals and five assists, Cash was a key component in Forest's push for the Play-Offs last season and it was of little surprise that he became a wanted man at Premier League level in the summer of 2020.

In September 2020, Cash sealed a transfer to Aston Villa which signalled the end of his Forest career. After stepping up to the Premier League, Cash reflected on his time with the Reds.

"Turning up at the City Ground as a 17-year-old lad, I always dreamed of playing there and to have five amazing years was a real honour.

"I have so many people to thank. Firstly the fans who have been absolutely remarkable, the manager and all his backroom staff, my teammates and a special mention to Gary Brazil for giving me the opportunity to play for Forest. There will always be a place in my heart for Forest."

SAMBA 21 SOW

POSITION: Midfielder **DOB:** 29/04/1989
COUNTRY: Mali

Following his summer signing from Dynamo Moscow, Mali international Samba Sow made his Forest debut in a 1-1 draw away to Leeds United in August 2019.

The 31-year-old midfielder went on to feature in a further 24 Championship fixtures in his maiden season at the City Ground. A tough tackling defensive midfielder, Sow began his career with French club Lens.

22 RYAN YATES

POSITION: Midfielder **DOB:** 21/11/1997
COUNTRY: England

Combative midfielder Ryan Yates enjoyed a continued taste of first team action for the Reds in 2019/20, making 28 appearances of which 27 were in Forest's Championship campaign.

Another product of the club's famed youth Academy, Yates has benefitted from loan spells with Shrewsbury Town, neighbours Notts County and Scunthorpe United ahead of making his mark at the City Ground.

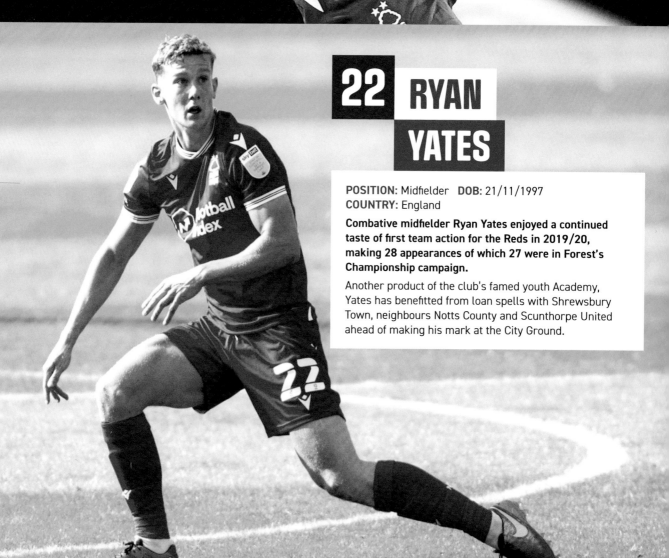

FOREST

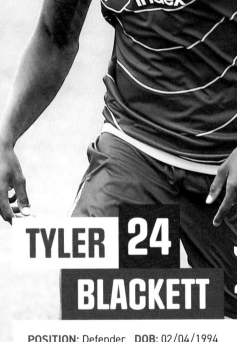

JOE 23 LOLLEY

POSITION: Midfielder **DOB:** 25/08/1992
COUNTRY: England

Forest's Player of the Season in 2018/19, Joe Lolley was once again a star performer at the City Ground in 2019/20 as the club mounted a sustained bid for the Play-Offs.

A real match winner, Lolley was signed from Huddersfield Town in January 2018 and brings both Championship and Premier League know-how to the Forest squad. A real favourite among the City Ground faithful, the 28-year-old reached double figures in the scoring charts last season from his 44 outings in all competitions.

TYLER 24 BLACKETT

POSITION: Defender **DOB:** 02/04/1994
COUNTRY: England

Former Manchester United defender Tyler Blackett joined Forest in the summer of 2020 having amassed over a century of league appearances with Reading.

A versatile defender, Blackett can operate comfortably at left-back or in central defence. He played a vital role in helping the Royals reach the 2016/17 Play-Off final and his arrival at the City Ground brings priceless experience to the Forest squad.

FOREST

There are five Robin Hoods hiding in the crowd as Nottingham Forest fans celebrate winning the FA Cup at Wembley in 1959. Can you find him?

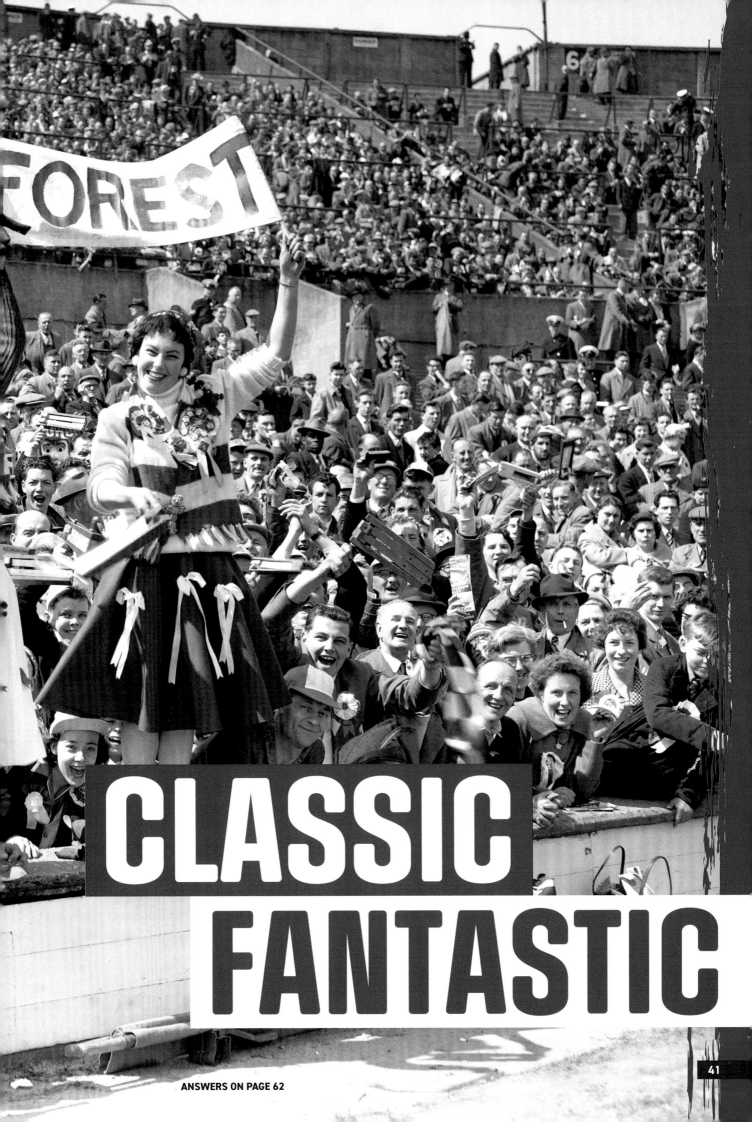

CLASSIC
FANTASTIC

ANSWERS ON PAGE 62

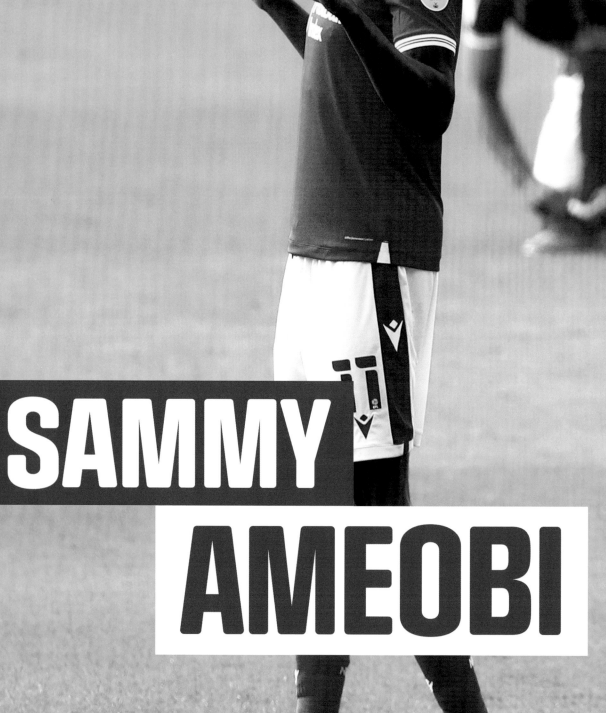

SAMMY
AMEOBI

42

Can you find the eight differences between these two photos?

SPOT THE DIFFERENCE

ANSWERS ON PAGE 62

2020/21

PREMIER LEAGUE

OUR PREDICTION FOR PREMIER LEAGUE WINNERS:
LEICESTER CITY

YOUR PREDICTION:

OUR PREDICTION FOR PREMIER LEAGUE RUNNERS-UP:
LIVERPOOL

YOUR PREDICTION:

CHAMPIONSHIP

OUR PREDICTION FOR CHAMPIONSHIP WINNERS:
NOTTINGHAM FOREST

YOUR PREDICTION:

OUR PREDICTION FOR CHAMPIONSHIP RUNNERS-UP:
SWANSEA CITY

YOUR PREDICTION:

TOP SCORERS

OUR PREDICTION FOR PREMIER LEAGUE TOP SCORER:
PIERRE-EMERICK AUBAMEYANG

YOUR PREDICTION:

OUR PREDICTION FOR CHAMPIONSHIP TOP SCORER:
LEWIS GRABBAN

YOUR PREDICTION:

FA CUP & EFL CUP

OUR PREDICTION FOR FA CUP WINNERS:
WATFORD

YOUR PREDICTION:

OUR PREDICTION FOR EFL CUP WINNERS:
BRIGHTON & HA

YOUR PREDICTION:

PREDICTIONS

SCOTT 26 McKENNA

POSITION: DEFENDER   **DOB:** 12/11/1996
COUNTRY: Scotland

Central defender Scott McKenna joined Nottingham Forest from Aberdeen in September 2020 after agreeing a four-year contract at the City Ground.

A full Scotland international, with a fantastic reputation north of the border, McKenna's move to Forest set a new 'club-record fee' for an Aberdeen sale. Alongside fellow new signing Harry Arter, McKenna made his Forest debut against Huddersfield Town on 25 September 2020.

FOREST

27 TENDAYI DARIKWA

POSITION: Defender   **DOB:** 13/12/1991
COUNTRY: Zimbabwe

Nottingham-born Tendayi Darikwa began his career with Chesterfield before the big defender stepped up to the Championship when he joined Burnley in 2015.

After two seasons at Turf Moor, Darikwa signed for Nottingham Forest and debuted in a 1-0 victory over Millwall at the City Ground in August 2017. He has now amassed over 60 first team appearances in a Forest shirt.

BRICE 30 SAMBA

POSITION: Goalkeeper   **DOB:** 25/04/1994
COUNTRY: France

Goalkeeper Brice Samba enjoyed an impressive debut season at the City Ground following his transfer from Caen in the summer of 2019.

Samba swiftly established himself as the Reds' first choice 'keeper and produced a number of eye-catching displays as Forest climbed the Championship table. He ended the 2019/20 campaign by being voted third in the fans' Player of the Season poll.

47

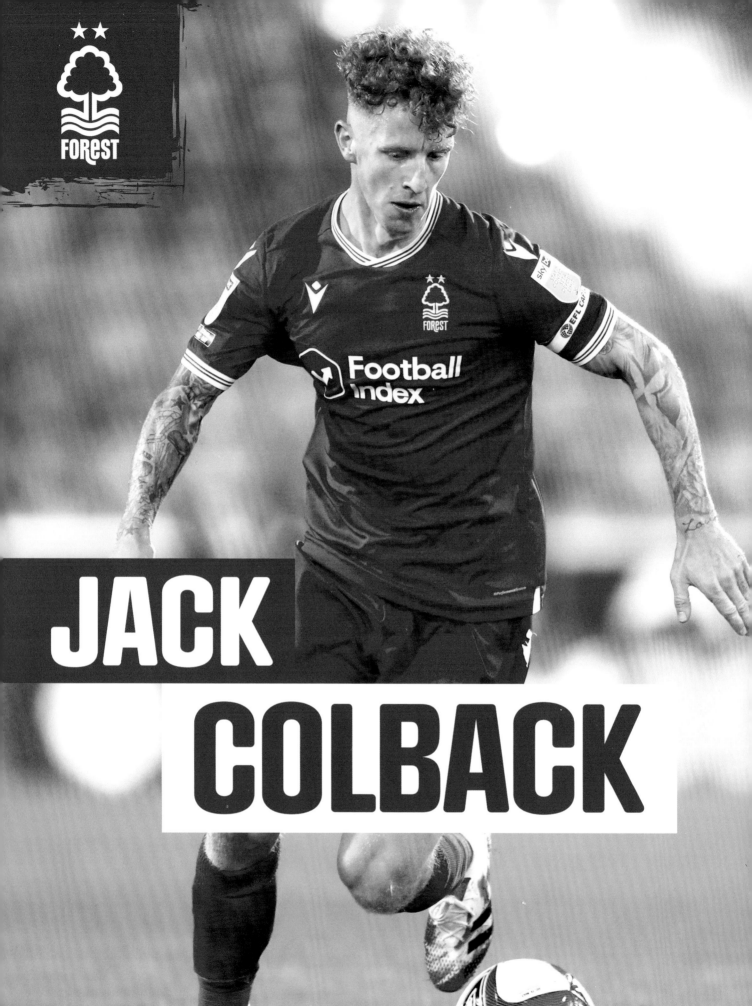

JACK

COLBACK

SOCCER SKILLS
CHEST CONTROL

Controlling the ball quickly and with minimum fuss in order to get the ball where you want it, so you can pass or shoot, can be the difference between a good player and a top class player.

EXERCISE ONE

Grab two of your mates to start the exercise. A and C stand 10yds apart and have a ball each, ready to act as servers.

B works first. B must run towards A who serves the ball for B to control with the chest and pass back to A. B then turns, runs to C and repeats the exercise.

Once B has worked for 30 seconds all the players rotate.

KEY FACTORS

1. Look to control the ball as early as possible.
2. Get in line with the ball.
3. Keep eyes on the ball.
4. Relax the body on impact with the ball to cushion it.

EXERCISE TWO

In this exercise there are 5 servers positioned around a 15yd square. At one side of the square there is a goal.

T starts in the middle of the square. S1 serves first, throwing the ball in the air towards T. T must control the ball with the chest and try to shoot past the goalkeeper, as soon as T has shot on goal they must prepare for the next serve from S2.

Once T has received a ball from every server the players rotate positions - the same key factors apply.

Players who can control a ball quickly, putting the ball in a position for a shot or pass, give themselves and their teammates the extra valuable seconds required in today's intense style of play.

49

Challenge your favourite grown-up and find out which of you is the biggest Championship brain!

FOREST

Prior to moving to the Madejski Stadium, where did Reading play their home matches?

11 ANSWER

Which kit manufacturer produces Queens Park Rangers' 2020/21 playing strip?

12 ANSWER

At which Championship club did Preston goalkeeper Declan Rudd begin his career?

13 ANSWER

What nationality is Millwall goalkeeper Bartosz Bialkowski?

14 ANSWER

At which club did Coventry City manager Mark Robins begin his managerial career?

15 ANSWER

Who did Garry Monk succeed as Sheffield Wednesday boss in 2019?

16 ANSWER

What was the name of Derby County's former ground?

17 ANSWER

Cardiff City midfielder Will Vaulks plays international football for which country?

18 ANSWER

Who is the captain of Stoke City?

19 ANSWER

From which club did Preston North End sign Scott Sinclair?

20 ANSWER

V KIDS

The adults' questions are on the left page and the kids' questions are on the right page.

Who is the manager of Reading?

11

Wayne Rooney plays for which Championship club?

12

With which country is Norwich goalkeeper Tim Krul a full international?

13

Which club's nickname is 'The Lions'?

14

Which country did Stoke City manager Michael O'Neill guide to finals of Euro 2016?

15

What nationality is Norwich City manager Daniel Farke?

16

Rammie and Ewie are the official mascots of which Championship club?

17

Queens Park Rangers are famous for playing in what type of shirts?

18

Which Championship team play their home matches at Ewood Park?

19

Who is the manager of Rotherham United?

20

ANSWERS ON PAGE 62

BOYS OF 1998

Nottingham Forest secured an immediate return to the Premier League as First Division Champions in 1997/98.

Having suffered relegation from the top flight the previous season along with Sunderland and Middlesbrough, Forest stormed to the First Division title under the management of Dave Bassett and secured the top slot with an impressive 94-point haul.

Promotion was achieved via a great team effort but the season is particularly remembered for the goalscoring partnership of Kevin Campbell and Pierre van Hooijdonk who fired home a combined tally of 52 league goals and often just proved too hot to handle for opposing defences.

STAR PERFORMER

PIERRE VAN HOOIJDONK

Pierre van Hooijdonk spearheaded Forest's 1997/98 campaign as the club secured an immediate return to the Premier League as First Division Champions.

Van Hooijdonk was signed in March 1997 following a highly successful spell in Scotland with Celtic. He arrived with Forest deep in relegation trouble and his signing was unable to spark an upturn in fortunes. Despite relegation from the Premier League, the Dutchman remained loyal to the club and was a star performer in the title success of 1997/98.

Forming an explosive strike partnership with Kevin Campbell, van Hooijdonk was joint leading goalscorer in the First Division, with his 29-goal haul only matched by Sunderland's Kevin Phillips.

The season began with Campbell on target in a 1-0 win away to Port Vale. By the end of the opening month of the campaign the two strikers were in fine form and had netted seven goals between them as Bassett's men took maximum points from their opening four league games.

The front pair complemented one another superbly and developed an almost telepathic understanding of one another's runs and movement. However, the team also benefitted greatly from the experience provided by veteran goalkeeper Dave Beasant and club stalwart Steve Chettle. While left-back Alan Rogers enjoyed an impressive debut season at the City Ground.

Unsurprisingly it was fellow relegated clubs, Sunderland and Middlesbrough who provided Forest's closest rivals for promotion but a run of five wins and two draws in their final seven games saw Basset's men top the pile.

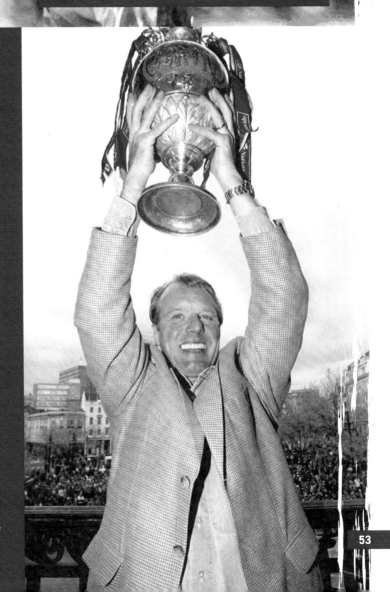

HARRY 31 ARTER

POSITION: Midfielder   **DOB:** 28/12/1989
COUNTRY: England

An all-action midfielder and Republic of Ireland international, Harry Arter joined Nottingham Forest from Championship rivals AFC Bournemouth with the 2020/21 campaign underway.

He agreed a three-year deal at the City Ground after spending the 2019/20 season on loan at Fulham, where he helped the Cottagers win promotion to the Premier League via the end-of-season Play-Offs. Arter debuted in Forest's televised match at Huddersfield on 25 September 2020.

33 LYLE TAYLOR

POSITION: Striker   **DOB:** 29/03/1990
COUNTRY: Montserrat

Nottingham Forest completed the signing of experienced striker Lyle Taylor in August 2020.

Taylor arrived at the City Ground following two outstanding seasons with Charlton Athletic. The 30-year-old striker netted 22 goals as Charlton won promotion to the Championship via the League One Play-Offs in 2018/19 and netted eleven goals in just 22 Championship outings for the Addicks last season.

TEAM 2020/21

39 ABDOULAYE DIALLO

POSITION: Goalkeeper **DOB:** 30/03/1992
COUNTRY: Senegal

Nottingham Forest added to their goalkeeping ranks with the signing of 28-year-old Senegal international Abdoulaye Diallo in September 2020.

The 'keeper moved to the City Ground as a free agent having left Turkish side Genclerbirligi. Diallo was a French Cup winner with Rennes in 2019.

NICOLAS 44 LOANNOU

POSITION: Defender **DOB:** 10/11/1995
COUNTRY: Cyprus

Cyprus international defender Nicolas Loannou completed a September 2020 transfer from APOEL to the City Ground. .

The 24-year-old defender is no stranger to England having spent eight years in the Manchester United youth system prior to returning to his native country with APOEL in 2014. He made his Forest debut against Bristol City on 3 October 2020.

JARGON BUSTER

Here is a list of footy jargon. All but one of the terms are hidden in the grid...

...can you work out which is missing?

All To Play For

Back Of The Net

Bags Of Pace

Big Game Player

Box-To-Box

Class Act

Derby Day

Dinked In

Early Doors

Funny Old Game

Game Of Two Halves

Handbags

Hat-Trick

Hollywood Pass

Keep It Tight

Massive Game

Midfield General

Natural Goalscorer

Row Z

Worldy

```
A S M Z U C E M A G E V I S S A M
V A W T B X O W A C V T S V Y B N
P O I B Y D I N K E D I N B R Q A
R L Q C J K X Z E F M L F J N E T
O G F W K C I R T T A H C S A Z U
E X B H D A V A P N H X G B J E R
T K A L L T O P L A Y F O R D C A
I R C P M E Q M O L R X G H O A L
F L K D N U R A S T T P K Q C P G
U F O N Z Y D I W O M W Y I B F O
N H F W Z O E S B B U N E H L O A
N J T G O B N O D F F X K A D S L
Y Z H S V R X M A G V O R N I G S
O X E A D C L H H G A E U D Z A C
L B N K Q J L D C J N K A B I B O
D D E R B Y D A Y E E S P A L B R
G W T E U O I P G J I O J G S M E
A C I O K I R D Y U X K T S F A R
M H W V Y B L T B P C H F O R R A
E O P C D E E T G E G Q B L P E N
V G C M I H A F M I E K Y V Z G L
H J B F D W A R T X I D H D C T D
L X D M O A S T A S O L G A T C R
V I A Q K Y I H S O D W J H Y A Q
M P F E Z P R G R G U N F M I S G
Z I N Q E J N S L J P I K Z Y S O
D B S E V L A H O W T F O E M A G
E K T X S L T E M X K W U L L I
U S N Q L U W E A B V R S P C O
A Y O R S F I T W Y O T A N B M
H O L L Y W O O D P A S S U T I
```

ANSWERS ON PAGE 62

LOIC
MBE SOH

Want to leap like Brice Samba, have the strength of Cyrus Christie or boast the endurance of Jack Colback? Build up your strength for action with our...

30 DAY

Day 1
Right let's get started! 10 squats, 25 star jumps, 10 sit-ups - all before school!

Day 2
Make your mum a brew before going out to practice your keepy-uppys

Day 3
10 squats
50 star jumps
10 sit-ups

Day 4
How about swapping the crisps in your lunchbox for an apple?

Day 5
Take a one mile ride on your bike

Day 6
75 star jumps
15 sit-ups
15 press-ups

Day 7
Help clean the car before going out to play headers and volleys with your friends

Day 8
75 star jumps
15 sit-ups
15 press-ups
Before and after school now!

Day 9
Walk to school rather than take the bus

Day 10
Head to the swimming pool for a 30-minute swim

Day 11
100 star jumps
20 sit-ups
20 press-ups
Twice a day now, don't forget!

Day 12
Make sure you trade one of your fizzy drinks for a glass of water today

Day 13
Jog to the shop for your mum... before playing any video games!

Day 14
Give a hand around the house before kicking your ball against the wall 500 times

Day 15
Time to increase those exercises!
25 squats
25 sit-ups
25 press-ups
Before and after school!

Day 16
Take a nice paced two-mile jog today

Day 17
25 squats
150 star jumps
25 press-ups
Remember, before and after school

Day 18
Cycle to school rather than rely on the bus or a lift

Day 19
30 squats
150 star jumps
30 press-ups
Twice a day too!

Day 20
Get out and practice those free-kicks, practice makes perfect remember...

Day 21
Get peddling! Time for a two-mile trip on two wheels today

Day 22
Upping the workload now...
40 squats, 40 sit-ups
40 press-ups
Before and after school!

Day 23
Wave goodbye to the chips - ask for a nice salad for lunch today

Day 24
40 squats
40 sit-ups
40 press-ups
Twice a day, don't forget...

Day 25
Time to get pounding the streets - the jogging is up to three miles today

Day 26
45 star jumps
45 sit-ups
45 press-ups

Day 27
Time to swap those sweets and biscuits for some fruit

Day 28
45 star jumps
45 sit-ups
45 press-ups

Day 29
You're getting fitter and fitter now! Keep up the squats and star jumps plus join an after-school sports club - ideally football!

Day 30
Well done - you made it!
50 squats, 50 sit-ups and 50 press-ups!
These are the core ingredients to your success

CHALLENGE
to improve your all-round footy fitness!

WHAT BALL?

Can you figure out what ball is the real one in each photo?

FOREST

TOBIAS
FIGUEIREDO

ANSWERS

PAGE 16 · ADULTS V KIDS

Adults

1. Blackburn Rovers. 2. Seven - Brentford, Bristol City, Luton Town, Millwall, Preston North End, Rotherham United and Wycombe Wanderers. 3. Jonny Howson. 4. Glasgow Rangers. 5. Middlesbrough. 6. Swansea City. 7. Nottingham Forest. 8. False. 9. Deepdale, Preston North End. 10. 2019.

Kids

1. Norwich City. 2. The Owls. 3. Coventry City and Rotherham United. 4. Bristol City. 5. Neil Harris. 6. Two, Cardiff City and Swansea City. 7. QPR. 8. Hillsborough, Sheffield Wednesday. 9. Seven - Birmingham City, Bristol City, Cardiff City, Coventry City, Norwich City, Stoke City and Swansea City. 10. Scottish.

PAGE 20 · WHO ARE YER?

1. Sammy Ameobi. 2. Ryan Yates.
3. Tyler Blackett. 4. Lewis Grabban.
5. Joe Worrall. 6. Brice Samba.
7. Tobias Figueiredo. 8. Lyle Taylor.
9. Jack Colback. 10. Luke Freeman.

PAGE 40
CLASSIC FANTASTIC →

PAGE 43
SPOT THE DIFFERENCE →

PAGE 50 · ADULTS V KIDS

Adults

11. Elm Park. 12. Errea. 13. Norwich City. 14. Polish. 15. Rotherham United. 16. Steve Bruce. 17. The Baseball Ground. 18. Wales. 19. Ryan Shawcross. 20. Celtic.

Kids

11. Veljko Paunovic. 12. Derby County. 13. Holland. 14. Millwall. 15. Northern Ireland. 16. German. 17. Derby County. 18. Blue and white hoops. 19. Blackburn Rovers. 20. Paul Warne.

PAGE 56 · JARGON BUSTER

Big Game Player.

PAGE 60 · WHAT BALL?

TOP: Ball D.
BOTTOM: Ball B.